LEVEL THREE

piano student

By David Carr Glover
and Louise Garrow

David Carr Glover
PIANO LIBRARY

MARVIN EDSON

The Piano Student - Level III
by
David Carr Glover
and
Louise Garrow

Foreword

This book is designed to follow logically "THE PIANO STUDENT", Level II, and continues to present attractive pieces and etudes.

More new keys are introduced and more new pieces are presented. The student now plays with ease the music in this book. Much attention is given to interpretation and tone quality. For additional materials at this level, refer to the "Teacher's Guide for David Carr Glover Piano Library."

Materials Correlated with "The Piano Student" — Level III

For additional solos and duets at this level, refer to the Program Solo and Ensemble Series listed in the "Teacher's Guide for David Carr Glover Piano Library."

Contents

4

The Red Drum
Interlocking Hands
Recital Solo

Playfully

GLOVER

YOU ARE NOW READY FOR A NEW BOOK "PIANO THEORY", DAVID CARR GLOVER PIANO LIBRARY, LEVEL III.

F.D.L.325

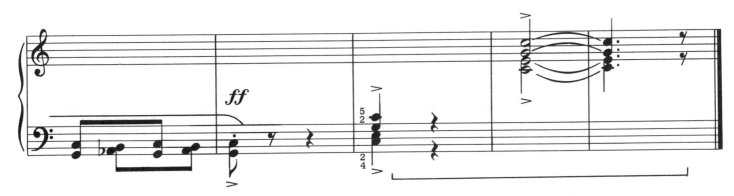

Triplets

A Triplet is a group of three notes played in the usual beat value of two similar notes.

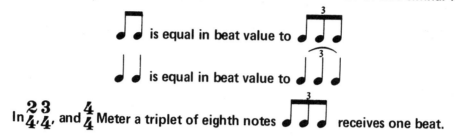

Clap and chant the following triplet rhythm pattern.

I. Beau-ti-ful Beau-ti-ful Beau-ti-ful day.   Beau-ti-ful Beau-ti-ful Beau-ti-ful day.

II. 1 - un - un 2 - oo - oo 3 - ee - ee 4   1 - un - un 2 - oo - oo 3 - ee - ee 4

YOU ARE NOW READY FOR A NEW BOOK "PIANO TECHNIC", DAVID CARR GLOVER PIANO LIBRARY, LEVEL III.

Happy Times

GLOVER

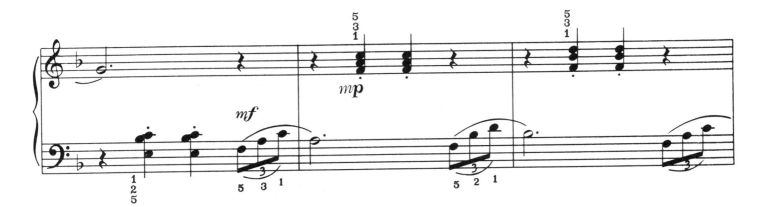

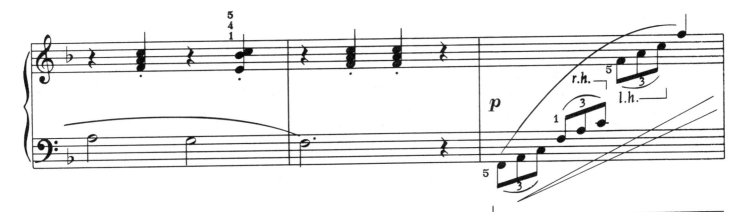

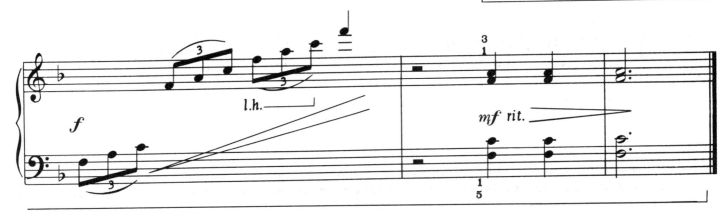

F.D.L. 325

The Coronation

GLOVER

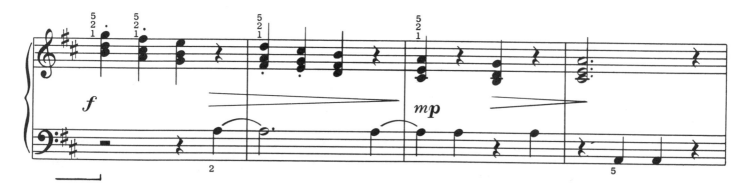

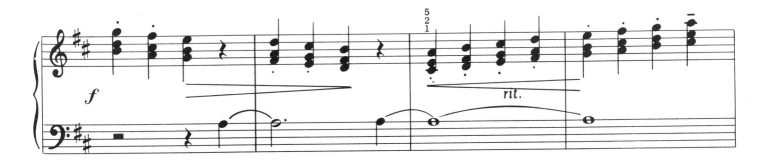

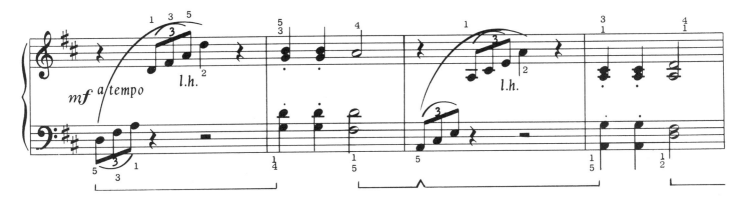

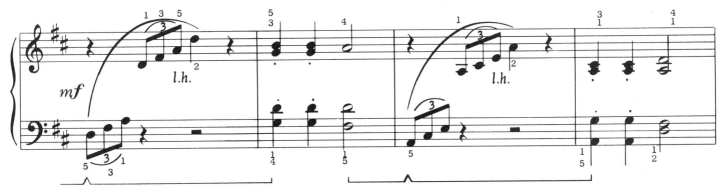

CODA

F.D.L. 325

"THE CHURCH MUSICIAN" LEVEL THREE FROM THE DAVID CARR GLOVER SACRED MUSIC PIANO LIBRARY IS RECOMMENDED AT THIS TIME. THIS IS A REPERTOIRE BOOK OF TRADITIONAL AND NEW RELIGIOUS MUSIC.

Paper Dragon Kite
(A Black Key Study)

GLOVER

Moving along but not fast

(Play all black notes staccato for a bell like tone)

Damper pedal down throughout —

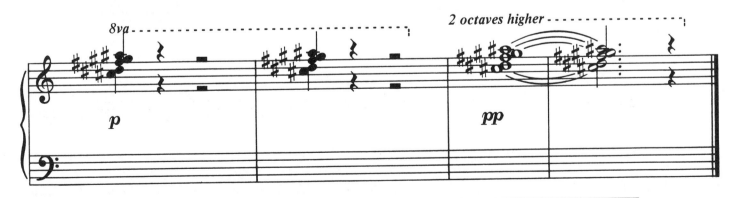

YOU ARE NOW READY FOR FOUR NEW SOLOS "AT THE BALLET", "DANCING BURRO", "WINDING RIVER",
and "THE GREAT CATHEDRAL".

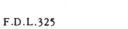

Major Triads

You have learned that when three notes of a scale are played together, they are called a CHORD.

A Major Triad is a three-note chord formed by playing the first, third, and fifth notes of the Major Scale.   The lowest note is the ROOT of the chord. The Major Triad has two whole steps between the Root and the middle note, and 1½ steps between the middle note and the top note.

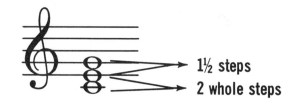

1½ steps
2 whole steps

Chord Inversions

The notes of a Triad in ROOT position are all line notes or all space notes. The ROOT or the name of the Triad is the lowest note. A Triad is INVERTED when the ROOT is on the top or in the middle.

C Major Triad and Inversions

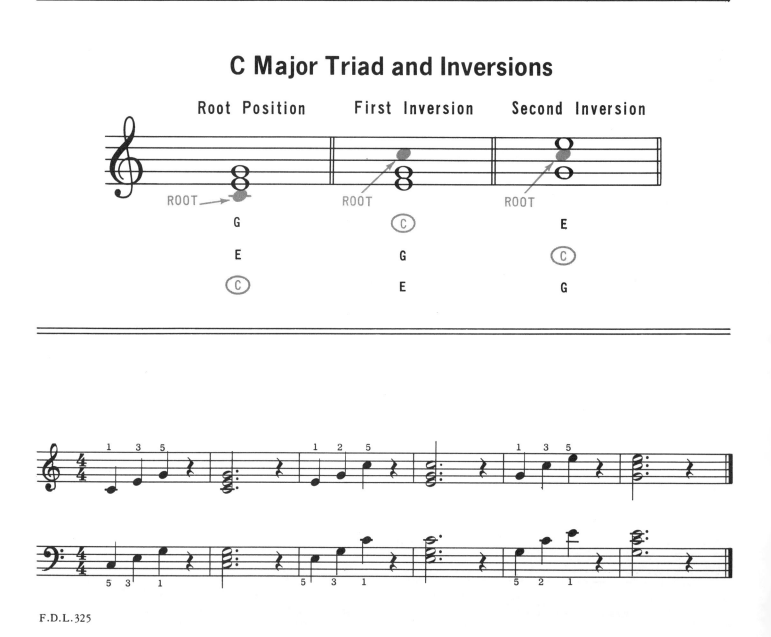

F Major Triad and Inversions

Root Position

ROOT

C
A
F

First Inversion

ROOT

F
C
A

Second Inversion

ROOT

A
F
C

G Major Triad and Inversions

Root Position

ROOT

D
B
G

First Inversion

ROOT

G
D
B

Second Inversion

ROOT

B
G
D

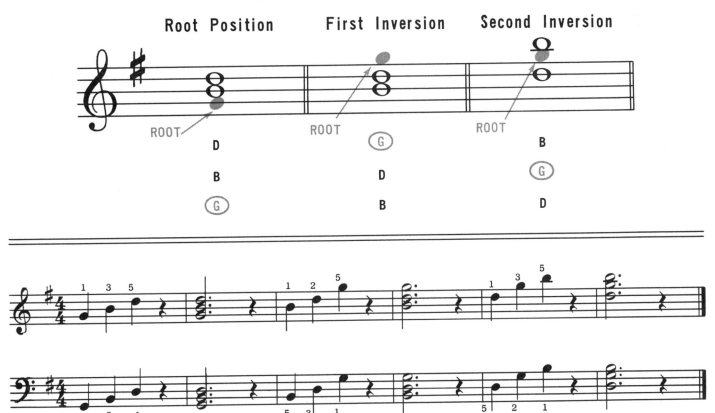

Major Chord Study

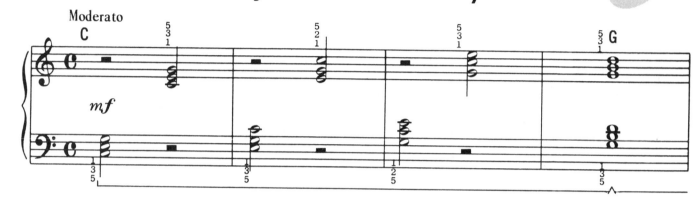

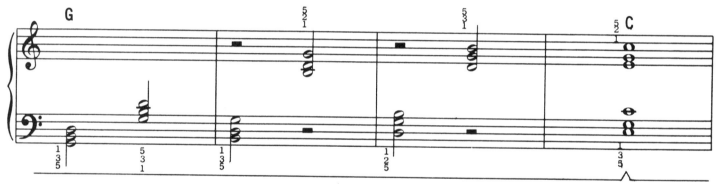

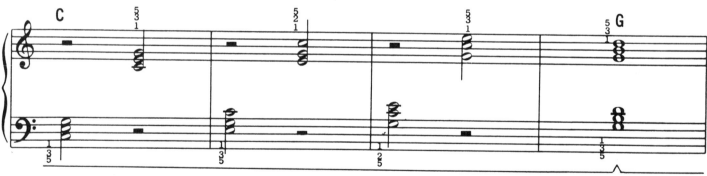

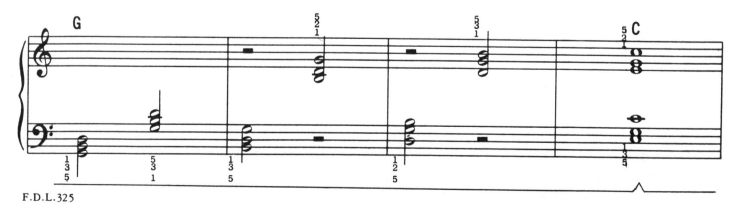

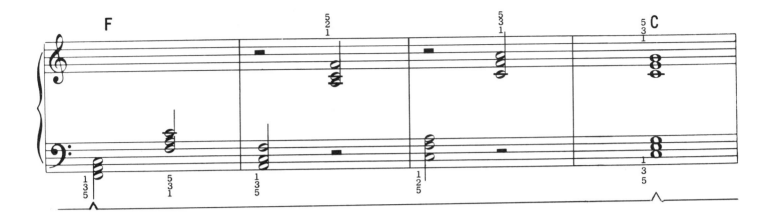

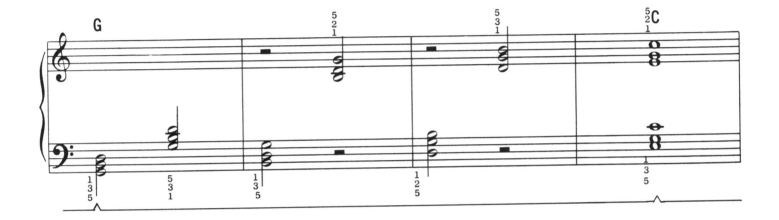

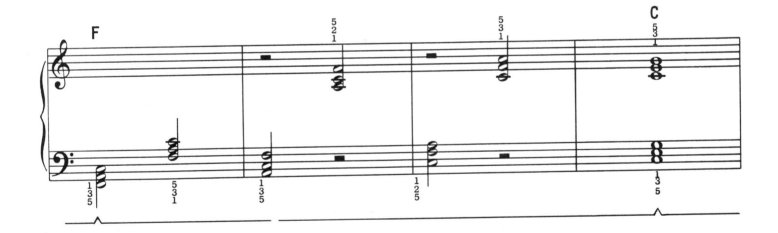

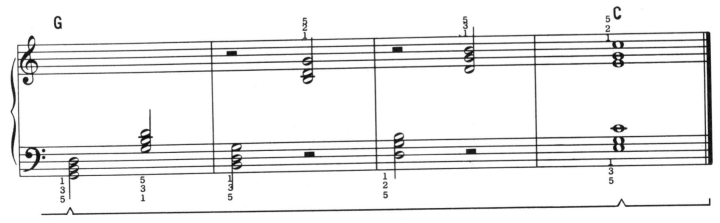

F.D.L.325

Transposing

The following chord study No. 1 is in the key of C Major. The same chord study No. 2 is in the key of D Major. You have learned that this is called TRANSPOSING. When you can play both keys as given, transpose the study into many other major keys.

NO. I

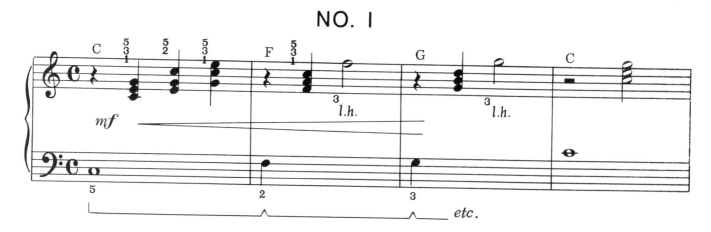

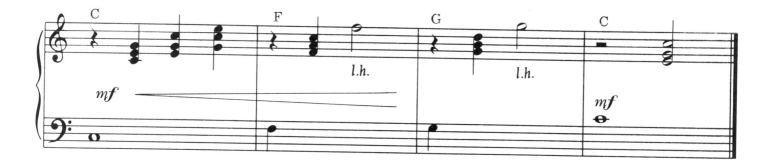

NO. II

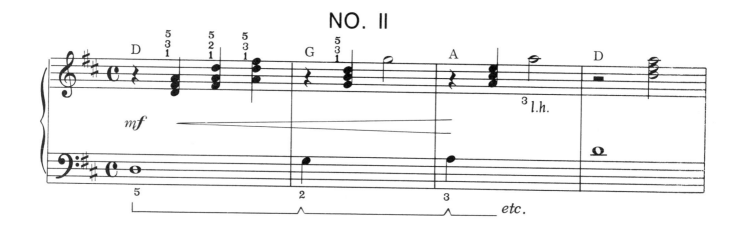

Leger Lines and Spaces

Leger lines and spaces are short lines and spaces added above and below the staff. They accommodate notes which are too high or low to be placed within the staff.

Write in names of notes.

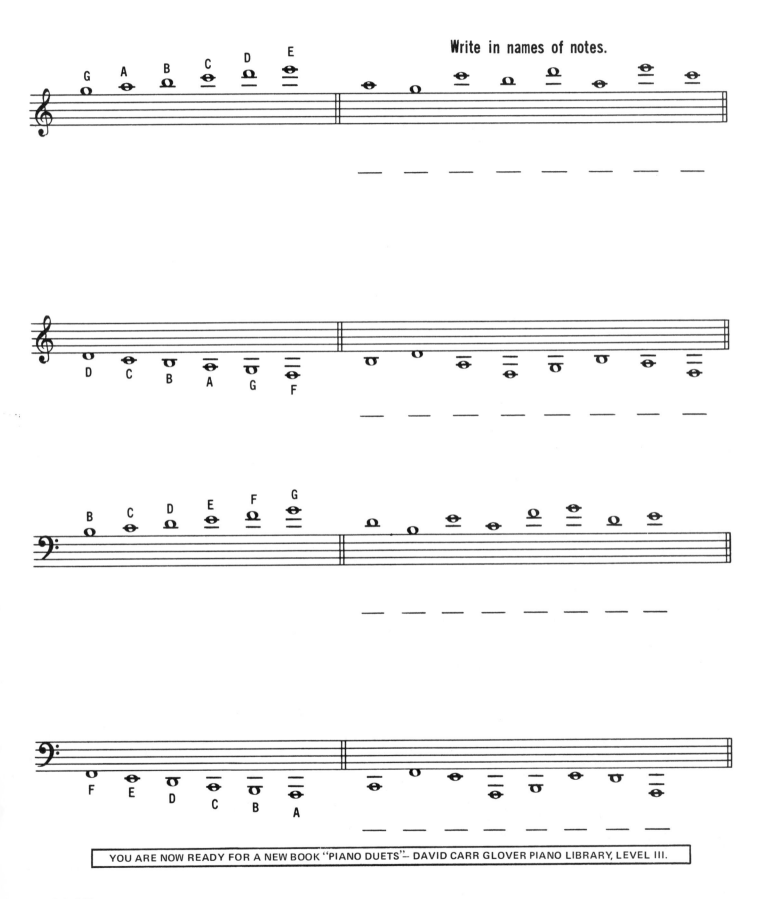

YOU ARE NOW READY FOR A NEW BOOK "PIANO DUETS"– DAVID CARR GLOVER PIANO LIBRARY, LEVEL III.

F.D.L.325

The Trumpeter

GURLITT

March tempo

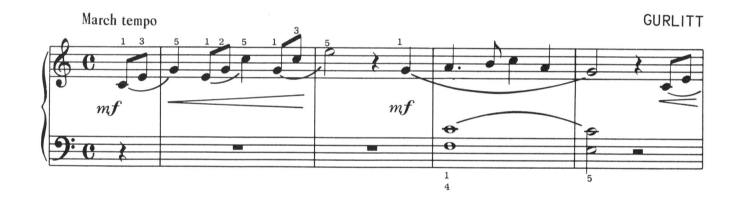

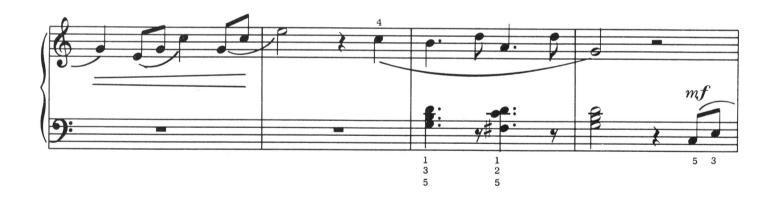

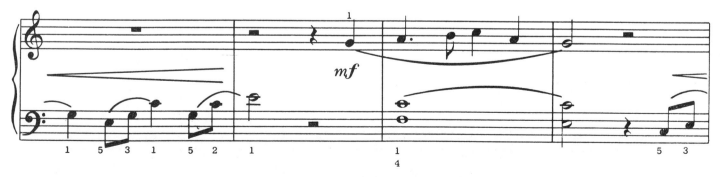

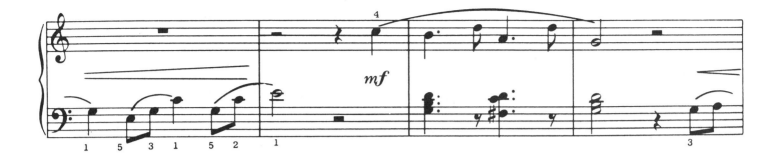

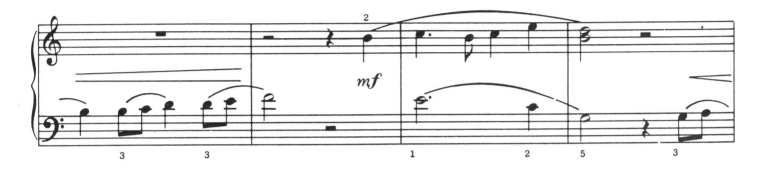

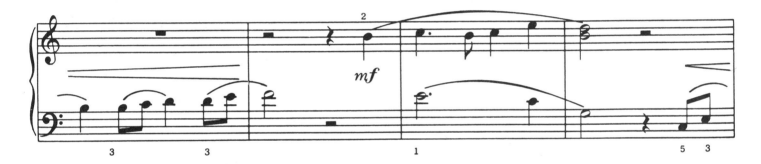

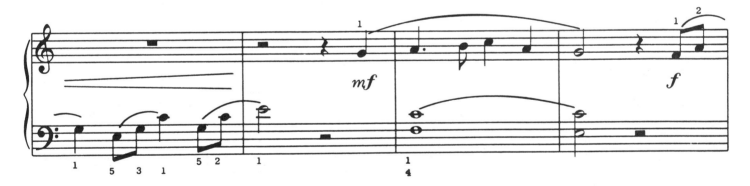

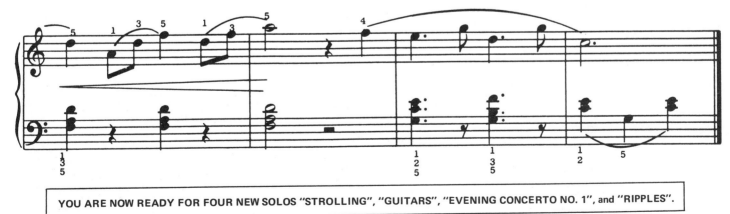

YOU ARE NOW READY FOR FOUR NEW SOLOS "STROLLING", "GUITARS", "EVENING CONCERTO NO. 1", and "RIPPLES".

F.D.L.325

Intervals

An Interval is the distance in pitch between two notes. The letter name of both the upper and lower notes are counted plus all the letter names in between.

Intervals of C Major Scale

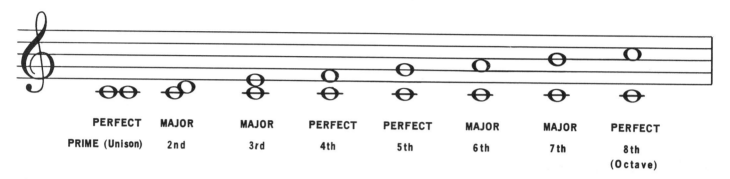

PERFECT	MAJOR	MAJOR	PERFECT	PERFECT	MAJOR	MAJOR	PERFECT
PRIME (Unison)	2nd	3rd	4th	5th	6th	7th	8th (Octave)

Interval Ear Training

As well as being able to recognize intervals on the printed page, it is most important to develop the ear to recognize intervals by their sound.

Circle the seconds in this piece, then play.

Circle the thirds, then play.

Circle the fourths, then play.

Circle the fifths, then play.

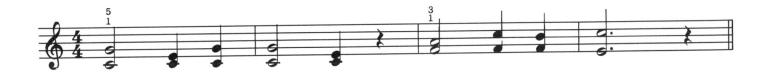

Circle the sixths, then play.

Circle the sevenths, then play.

Circle the eighths (octaves), then play.

F.D.L.325

Evening Song

KOHLER, OP. 216

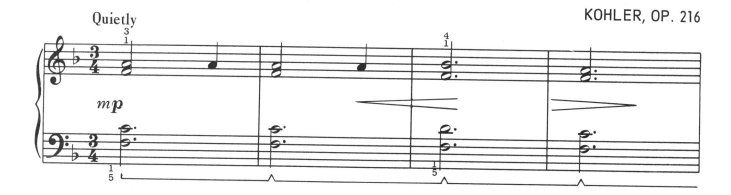

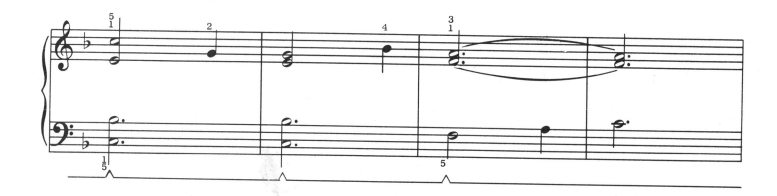

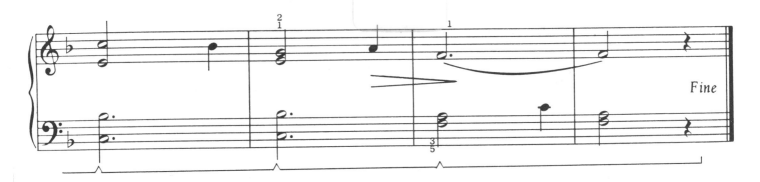

Fine

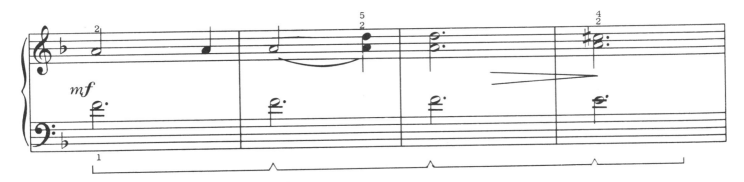

mp

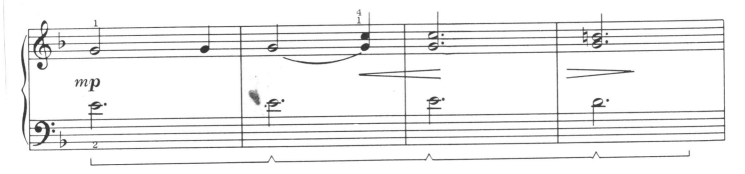

mf

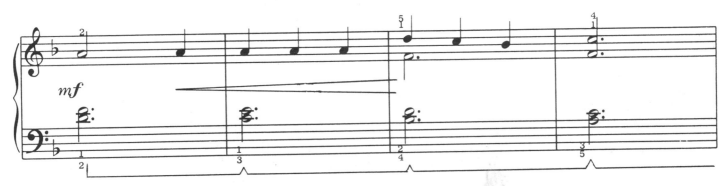

mf

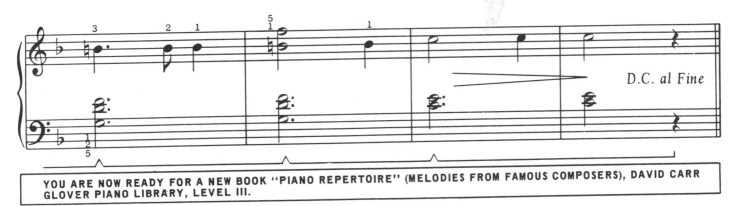

D.C. al Fine

YOU ARE NOW READY FOR A NEW BOOK "PIANO REPERTOIRE" (MELODIES FROM FAMOUS COMPOSERS), DAVID CARR GLOVER PIANO LIBRARY, LEVEL III.

F.D.L.325

Relative Minor Scales

The Relative Minor Scale is formed by beginning on the sixth tone (note) of the Major Scale.

> The Key Signature of the Relative Minor Scale is the same as its Relative Major.

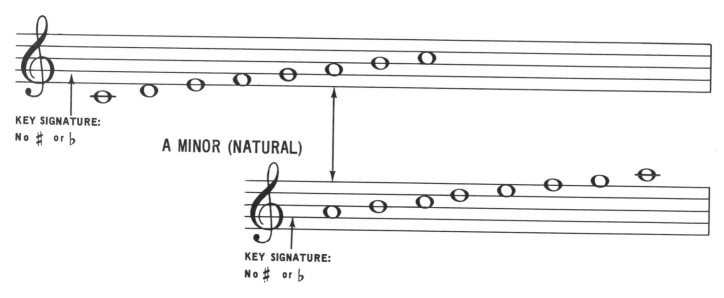

C MAJOR

KEY SIGNATURE:
No # or ♭

A MINOR (NATURAL)

KEY SIGNATURE:
No # or ♭

Forms of the Minor Scales

1. NATURAL — All notes of this scale are the same as its relative major (see above).

2. HARMONIC — The 7th tone (note) of the Natural Minor is raised ½ step.

> The raised 7th tone in the Harmonic Minor Scale is not included in the key signature.

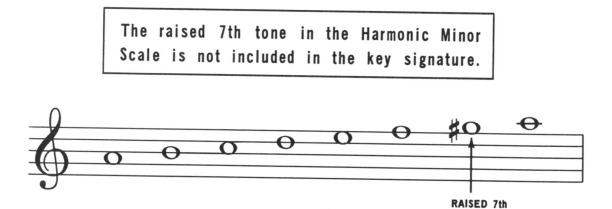

RAISED 7th

F.D.L.325

3. MELODIC — The 6th and 7th tones (notes) of the Natural Minor are raised ½ step each ascending, then lowered descending.

> The raised 6th and 7th tones in the Melodic Minor Scale are not included in the key signature. ★

★ ACCIDENTALS: Sharps and Flats not appearing in the key signature.

Parallel Minor Scales

When the Minor Scale begins on the same key note as the Major Scale, it is called the Parallel Minor.

> The key signatures of Parallel Minor and Major Scales are different.

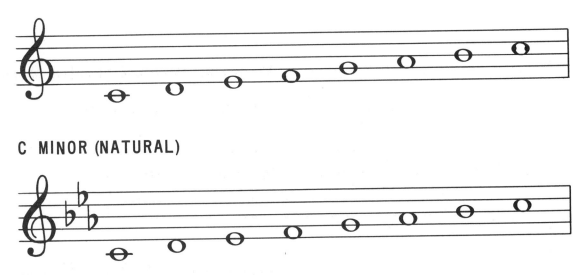

C MAJOR

C MINOR (NATURAL)

Parallel Harmonic and Melodic Minor Scales are formed the same way as Relative Harmonic and Melodic Minor Scales.

Minor Triads

A Minor Triad is a three note chord formed by playing the first, third, and fifth notes of the Minor Scale. The lowest note is the ROOT of the chord. The Minor Triad has 1½ steps between the Root and the middle note, and 2 whole steps between the middle note and the top note.

Minor Triads may also be formed by lowering the middle note of a Major Triad ½ step.

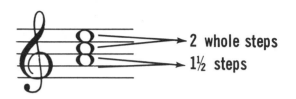

A Minor Triad and Inversions

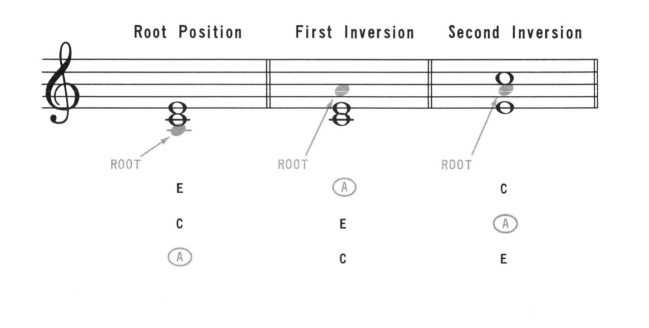

Minor Chord Study

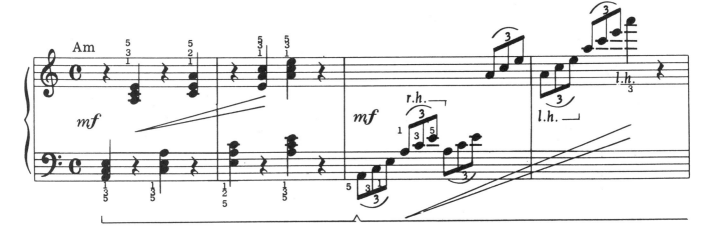

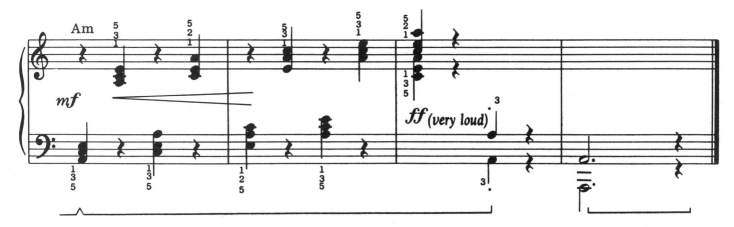

In the following solo you will

use both Soft and Damper pedals.

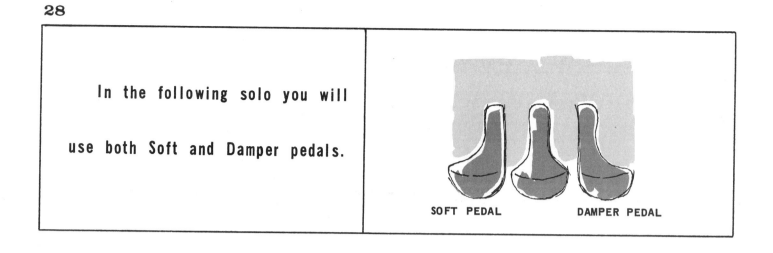

SOFT PEDAL   DAMPER PEDAL

Oasis

GLOVER

Slow and mysteriously

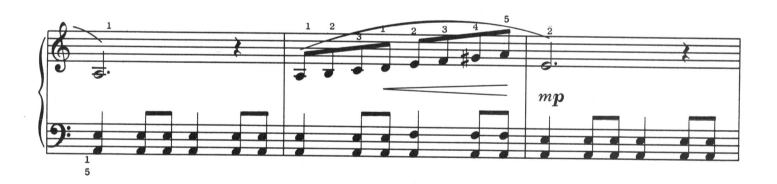

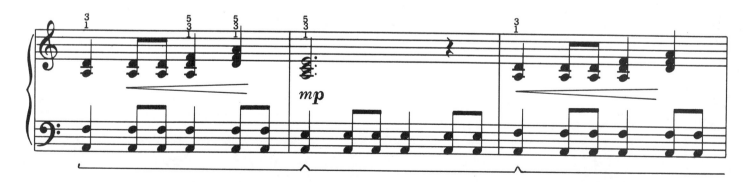

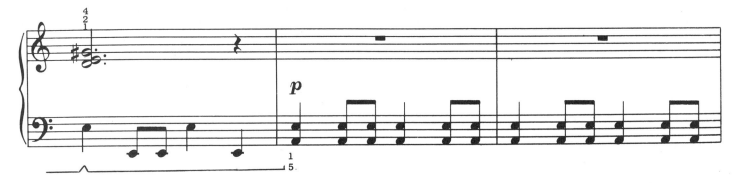

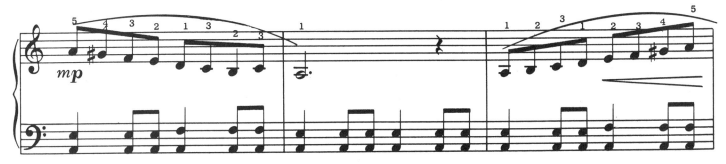

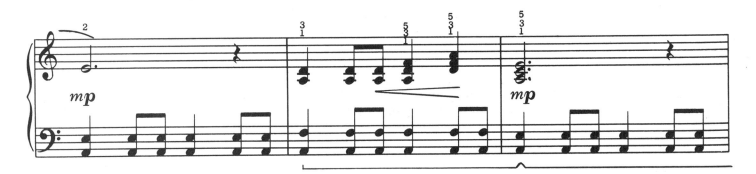

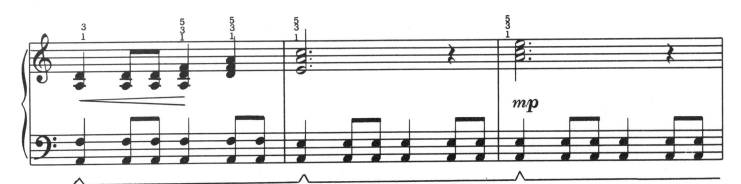

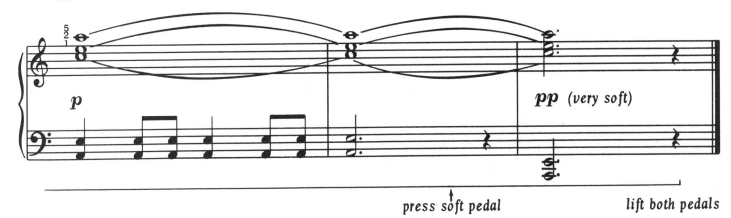

press soft pedal

lift both pedals

Franz Joseph Haydn was one of a large family of twelve children. He was a fun-loving child who liked to play pranks on his friends. Although his parents were poor, he managed to get a good musical education and later became a member of Count Esterhazy's household — a position which allowed him much time for composing. He wrote a great deal of beautiful music — string quartets, operas, sonatas and many symphonies. His happy, cheerful disposition is reflected in the quality of his music.

FRANZ JOSEPH HAYDN
1732 – 1809

Practice the left hand separately until the sustained bass voice is under control.

Quick Dance

HAYDN

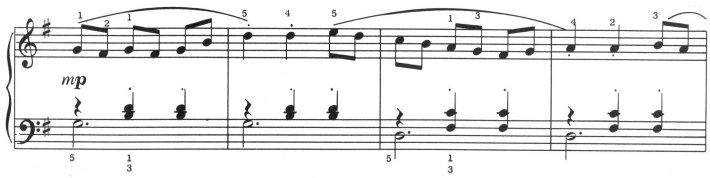

F.D.L.325

YOU ARE NOW READY FOR FOUR NEW SOLOS "COOL BLUE", "MEXICAN SERENADE", "HULA DANCERS", and "COMMANDOS".

ADDITIONAL SUSTAINED ACCOMPANIMENT STUDIES WILL BE FOUND ON PAGE 27 "PIANO TECHNIC" LEVEL III, DAVID CARR GLOVER PIANO LIBRARY.

THEME AND VARIATIONS

In the following Russian Folk Song, Minka, the melody is presented in its original form, then repeated twice with changes in rhythm and mood. This form of writing is known as Theme and Variations.

Minka

FOLK SONG
arr. GLOVER

Lively but not too fast

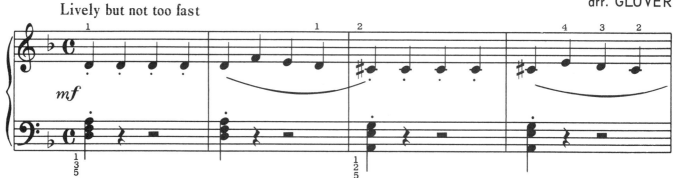

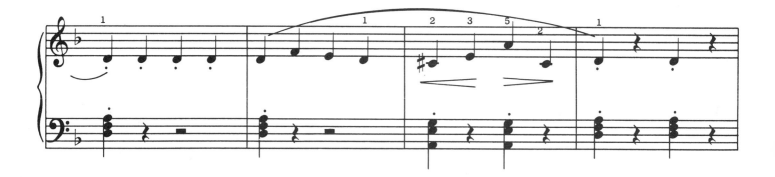

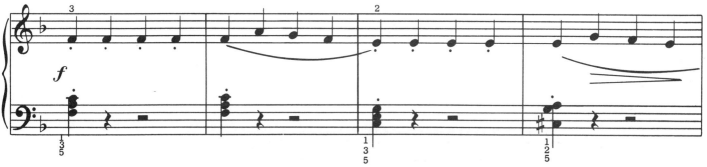

Slowly

rit.

Lively but not too fast

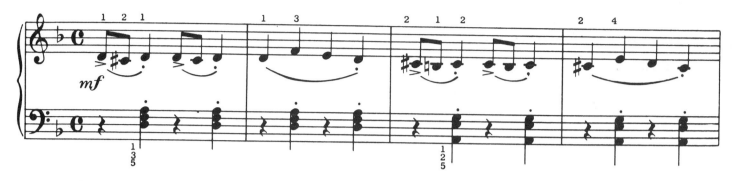

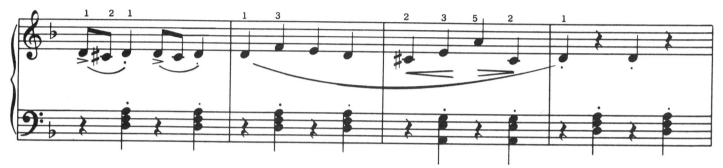

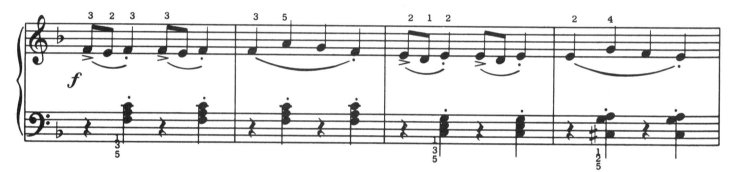

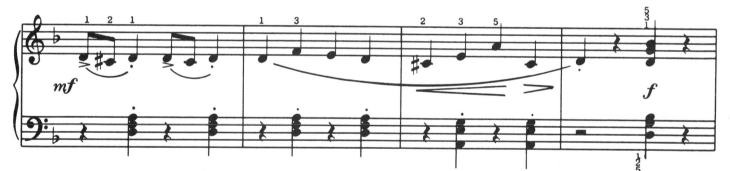

YOU ARE NOW READY FOR A NEW BOOK "JAZZ ON 88 (etc.)", DAVID CARR GLOVER PIANO LIBRARY, LEVEL III.

Edvard Grieg was born in Bergen, Norway, where today he is a national hero. There was a folk-like quality in all of his works and his music brought to the world the picture of Norway's beautiful lakes, valleys, and forests. The Concerto in A Minor for piano and orchestra is one of Grieg's most outstanding compositions.

EDVARD GRIEG
1843 - 1907

A CONCERTO is a large work for the orchestra and a single solo instrument. It usually has three contrasting parts or "movements".

Theme from Concerto in A Minor

GRIEG
arr. GLOVER

Broadly (not fast)

Moderato

Cantabile (in a singing style)

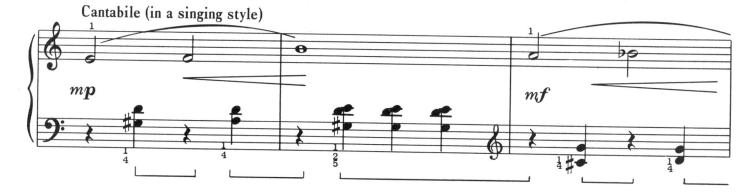

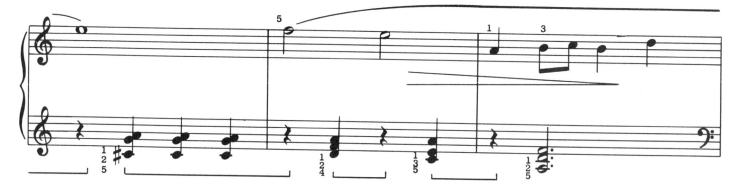

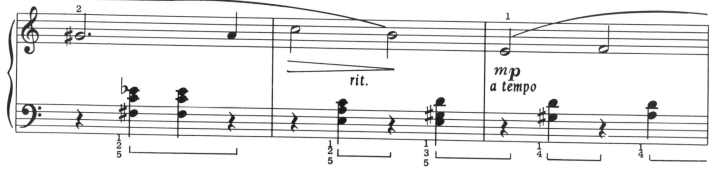

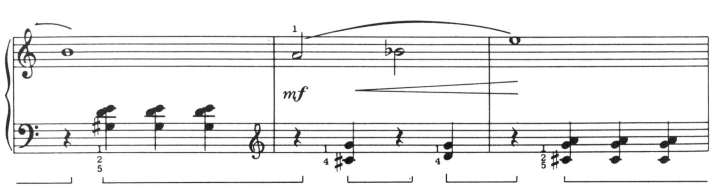

YOU ARE NOW READY FOR FOUR NEW SOLOS "HOE-DOWN", "CLOUDS", "DESERT SAND", and "CANDLELIGHT SUPPER CLUB".

Kabalevsky is a noted Russian composer. He was born in St. Petersburg and has been studying music and composing since the age of fourteen. His works include concertos, opera, symphonies, string quartets, ballet, and many works for the piano. His style is marked by clear tonality and energetic rhythms.

DMITRI BORISOVITCH KABALEVSKY
1904 –

Lament

KABALEVSKY

Moderately slow

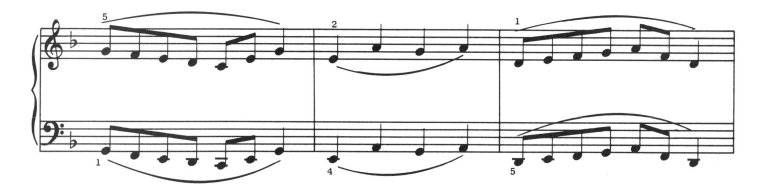

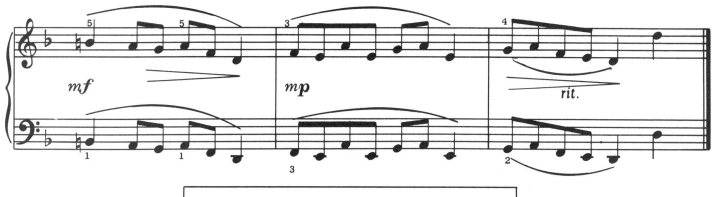

YOU ARE NOW READY FOR A NEW DUET "DUELING PIANO".

F.D.L.325

Peasant Dance

KABALEVSKY

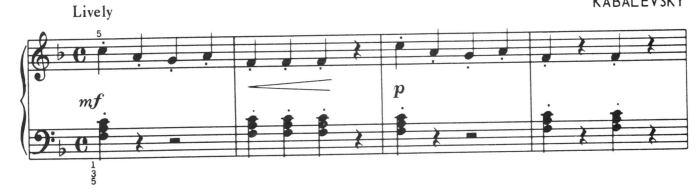

YOU ARE NOW READY FOR TWO NEW BOOKS, "THE HALF FILLED COOKIE JAR", and "THE SUNNY SNOW BEAR" DAVID CARR GLOVER PIANO LIBRARY, LEVEL III.

F.D.L.325

Cadence Chords

You have learned the principal chords of several keys. These chord progressions are called CADENCES. Cadence chords are very helpful in understanding the structure of music. There are many different kinds of Cadences. Below are some examples. Roman numerals indicate what degree of the scale the chord is built on. Chord letter names have been added.

Play each Cadence three times:
1. Right Hand only.   2. Left Hand only.   3. Both Hands together.

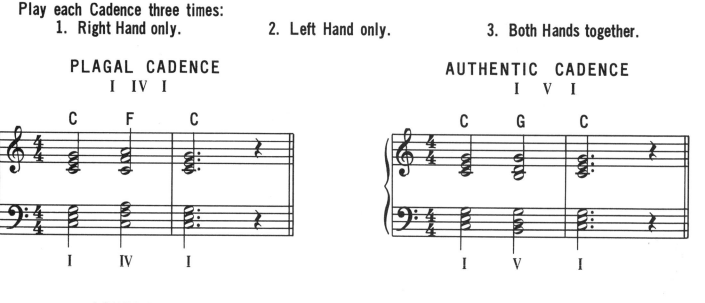

COMPLETE CADENCE OF C MAJOR IN THREE POSITIONS

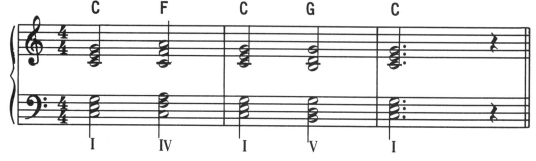

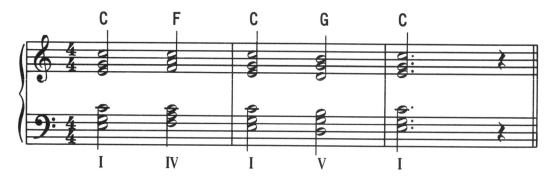

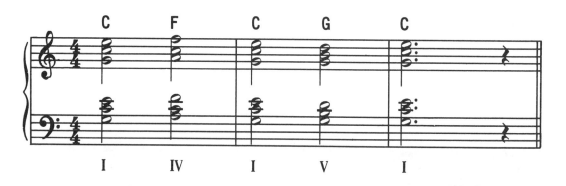

Minor Cadence Chords

Roman numerals indicate what degree of the scale the chord is built on. Chord letter names have been added. A small m means the chord is minor.

Note that the V Chord in a Minor Cadence is Major.

Play each Cadence three times:

    1. Right Hand only.   2. Left Hand only.   3. Both Hands together.

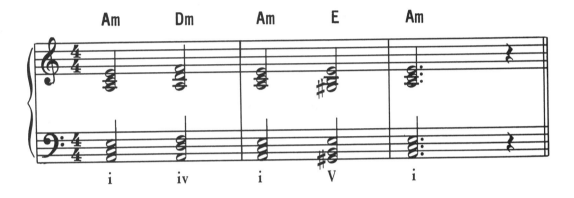

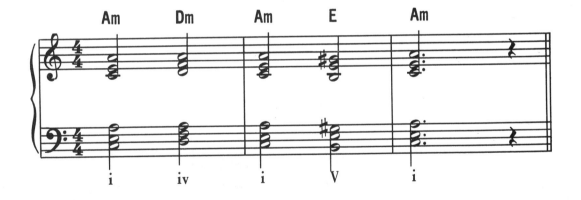

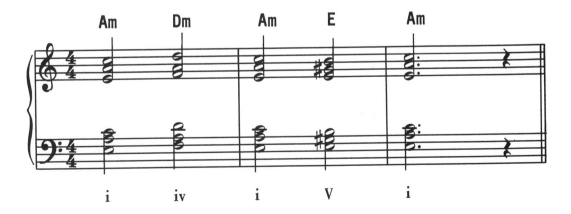

V7 Chord

For a richer V Chord we will add another note to the Triad which is a seventh from the Root. This seventh tone is 1½ steps above the top note of the Triad.

We have used the V7 Chord when we played the principal chords in various keys. At that time it was inverted and one note was omitted for clarity.

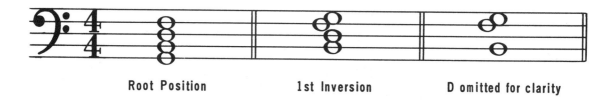

I V7 I Cadence Chords in the Key of C Major

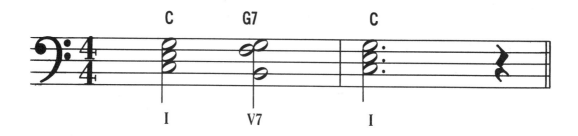

I V7 I Cadence in the Key of C Minor

The small letter m next to the chord letter name indicates that the chord is minor.

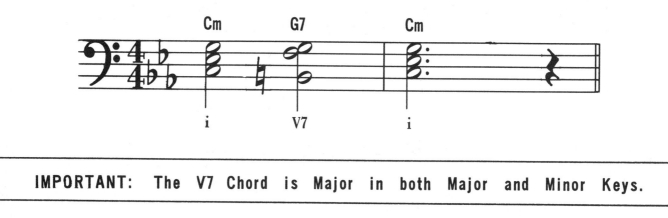

IMPORTANT: The V7 Chord is Major in both Major and Minor Keys.

I V7 I Cadence in Major Keys

The I V7 I CADENCES on this page will be most helpful for reference when harmonizing transposed melodies or harmonizing melodies when chord symbols are given. Refer to "Sacred Music" by Louise Garrow, Level II - David Carr Glover Piano Library.

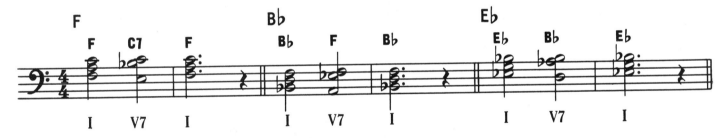

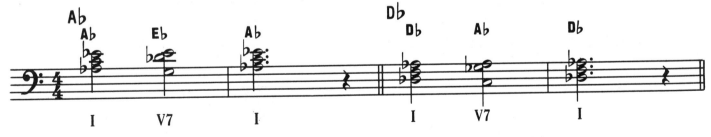

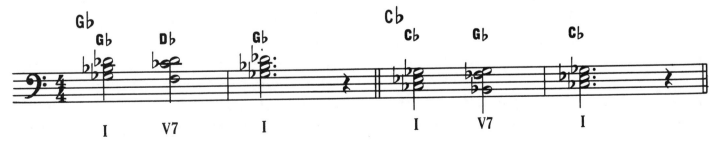

F.D.L.325

Key Signatures

Major Name of Key	Signature		Relative Minor Name of Key
C	No sharps or flats		a
G	F#		e
D	F# C#		b
A	F# C# G#		f#
E	F# C# G# D#		c#
B	F# C# G# D# A#		g#
F#	F# C# G# D# A# E#		d#
C#	F# C# G# D# A# E# B#		a#

F.D.L. 325

Key Signatures

Major Name of Key	Signature		Relative Minor Name of Key
F	B♭		d
B♭	B♭ E♭		g
E♭	B♭ E♭ A♭		c
A♭	B♭ E♭ A♭ D♭		f
D♭	B♭ E♭ A♭ D♭ G♭		b♭
G♭	B♭ E♭ A♭ D♭ G♭ C♭		e♭
C♭	B♭ E♭ A♭ D♭ G♭ C♭ F♭		a♭

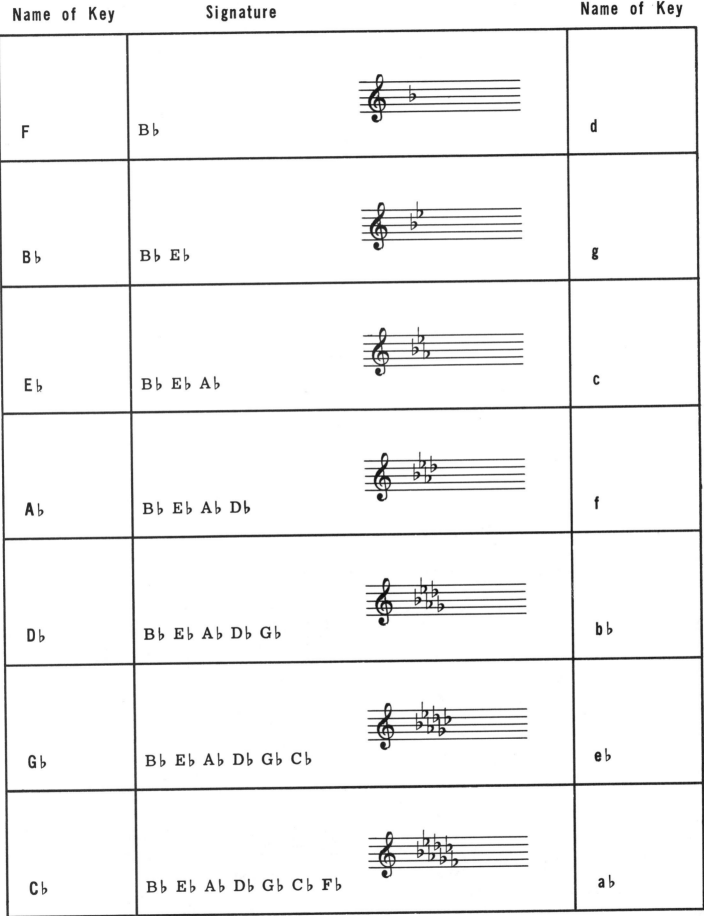

F.D.L.325

Musical Dictionary

Musical Term	Abbreviation	Definition
A Tempo		In time.
Accelerando	Accel.	Gradually increase speed.
Accent Mark	>	To make louder.
Alla marcia		In march time.
Allegretto		A little slower than Allegro.
Allegro		Fast, brisk.
Andante		A walking speed.
Animato		Lively.
Cantabile		In a singing style.
Con brio		With spirit.
Crescendo	Cresc.	Gradually growing louder.
Da Capo al Fine	D. C. al Fine	Return to the beginning and play to the word "Fine".
Dal Segno al Fine	D. S. al Fine	Return to the sign (%) and play to the word "Fine".
Decrescendo	Decresc.	Gradually growing softer.
Diminuendo	Dim.	Gradually growing softer.
Dolce		Sweetly, softly
Espressivo		With expression.
Fermata	⌒	Hold or pause.
Fine		The end.
Forte	f	Loud.
Fortissimo	ff	Very loud.
Grazioso		Gracefully.
Legato		Smooth and connected.
Marcato		Strongly marked.
Mezzo forte	mf	Moderately loud.
Mezzo piano	mp	Moderately soft.
Misterioso		With an air of mystery.
Moderato		A moderate speed.
8va		When 8va is placed over a note, play 8 keys (one octave) higher — under a note, play 8 keys lower.
Piano	p	Soft.
Pianissimo	pp	Very soft.
Poco a poco		Little by little.
Presto		Very fast.
Ritardando	rit.	Gradually slowing down.
Scherzando		Playfully.
Sforzando	sfz	With a strong accent.
Simile		Continue as indicated.
Slight Accent	—	Sustain the tone slightly.
Staccato	Stacc.	Short, disconnected.
Tempo		Speed.
Vivace		With life - fast.

Certificate of Award

THIS IS TO CERTIFY THAT

HAS COMPLETED

PIANO STUDENT

LEVEL THREE

OF THE

David Carr Glover
PIANO LIBRARY

Date

Teacher

F.D.L.325